Protecting the Islands

by Karen Alexander

CHAPTER 1

A Special Place

A shark swims through Maro Reef. It hunts for food. Birds dive into the water. They look for fish to eat.

Squirrelfish swimming through the coral

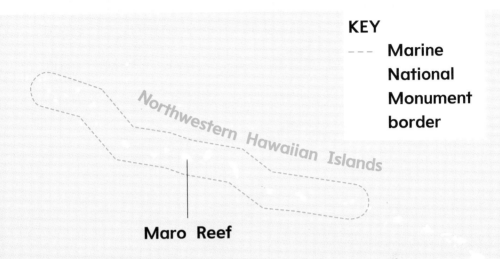

KEY

--- Marine National Monument border

Northwestern Hawaiian Islands

Maro Reef

The islands and waters of the NWHI Marine National Monument

Maro Reef is in the Northwestern Hawaiian Islands. Many animals live there. Some animals are **threatened**. Some might die out. The islands are a national monument. Everything there is **protected**.

3

National monuments show that a place is special. Some are buildings. Some are natural. This monument is very big. Thousands of animals live there. This is the only place in the world that some of these animals live.

No one lives on the islands.

STOP AND CHECK

Why is this national monument important to the animals there?

CHAPTER 2

The Coral Reef

There are many coral reefs here. They are full of plants and animals. The monument protects these plants and animals.

The coral reefs are in danger. Pollution can hurt the coral. Many reef fish are dying.

©James D. Watt/SeaPics.com

A bluefin trevally in the coral reef

The monument protects the coral reefs. People need **permission** to visit. No one can fish there. The reefs are kept safe.

Coral needs air, food, light, and water. It is made of tiny animals! It is important to save the coral reefs. The animals **depend** on each other to **survive**.

Millions of tiny animals make up coral. The animals make limestone from the water.

Some fish in the reef eat marine plants. These plants live in the ocean. The fish keep the plants from growing too big.

Other fish are predators. They eat other fish. Large predators like sharks keep the fish **population** down.

STOP AND CHECK

Why is it important to protect the coral reef?

The gray reef shark is a predator.

CHAPTER 3

Marine Nursery

Birds nest on the islands. They lay their eggs there. The monument protects these nesting places.

Black-footed albatrosses live there. Short-tailed albatrosses are their **relatives**. They also build nests there.

Albatross with chick

A short-tailed albatross and its chicks

These birds are endangered. In the past, many have been killed.

Most nesting areas of the short-tailed albatross have gone. The birds need safe places to nest.

Green Turtles

Turtles nest on the island, too. In the past, turtles were killed. Hunters wanted their meat and shells. Today, Hawaiian green turtles are endangered.

The monument protects turtles. There are no people on the islands. Turtles can lay their eggs safely.

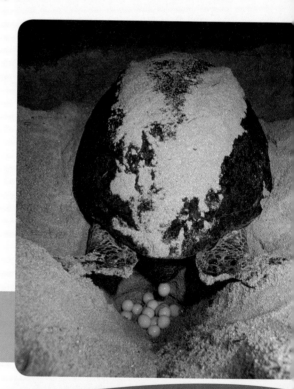

A green turtle and its eggs

Green turtles nest on the same beach every year.

Green turtles warm up in the sun. They come on land to nest. They eat plants. Their beaks have **rough** edges. They use their beaks to get plants off rocks.

STOP AND CHECK

Why are Hawaiian green turtles endangered?

CHAPTER 4

Animals and People

Hawaiian monk seals are also endangered. Most seals live in cold water. These seals live in warm water. They eat lobsters, eels, and fish.

Hawaiian monk seal

Yusuke Okada/a.collectionRF/amana images/Getty Images

Monk seals are not afraid of people. This can be **dangerous**. People come too close. The seals can catch **diseases**.

Most monk seals live in the monument. They are protected there.

Monk seal pups are born with black fur. They grow gray fur at six weeks old.

Many people are saving endangered animals. They fix beaches. They protect nesting areas. They try to keep oceans clean. They are **caretakers** for the world's **resources**.

Monuments are special places. Monuments help save the animals living there.

Fishers tie streamers to their lines. Birds are scared away. This saves their lives.

STOP AND CHECK

Why are people a threat to monk seals?

NOAA

Respond to Reading

Summarize

What have you learned about animals that are in danger? Use details from *Protecting the Islands* to summarize. Your chart may help you.

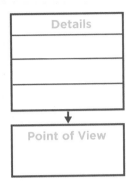

Text Evidence

1. Why do you think the author wrote this book? Point of View

2. Find the word *marine* on page 7. What does it mean? What clues help you figure it out? Vocabulary

3. Write about why birds can nest safely on the islands. Write About Reading

Compare Texts
Read how one person is helping
to save a threatened animal.

Penguins
Go Global

Dr. Borboroglu loves penguins. He cares for penguin nesting places.

Many dangers threaten penguins. Penguins must work hard to find fish. Oceans are warming. Oil and waste cause pollution.

Dr. Pablo Borboroglu

Some penguins are losing their homes. People build where penguins nest.

The health of penguins is important. We can learn about the health of oceans. Penguins run, jump, and swim. They need oceans to survive. Everything about the ocean affects penguins.

Penguins are good swimmers.

Dr. Borboroglu is protecting penguins. His work helps all marine animals.

Visitors like to watch penguins. Dr. Borboroglu teaches people to enjoy penguins without harming them.

Penguins are fun!

Make Connections

In *Penguins Go Global*, what is Dr. Borboroglu doing for penguins? **Essential Question**

In *Protecting the Islands* and *Penguins Go Global*, how do people work together to solve problems? **Text to Text**

Focus on
Science

Purpose To find out about a threatened animal

What to Do

Step 1 Choose a threatened animal that you are interested in.

Step 2 Find out as much as you can about the animal—where it lives, what it eats, and the threats to its survival.

Step 3 Make a chart headed "Threats."

Step 4 Write the threats faced by your animal in the chart.

Conclusion What could people do to help your animal?